We Go!

Trains

Dana Meachen Rau

Marshall Cavendish
Benchmark
New York

We go on a train.

3

Trains go on tracks.

Trains go on bridges.

Trains go in tunnels.

9

Trains go to stations.

Trains have windows.

Trains have rail cars.

Trains have beds.

We go on a train!

19

Words to Know

bed

bridge

rail cars

station

tracks

tunnels

windows

21

Index

Page numbers in **boldface** are illustrations.

About the Author

Dana Meachen Rau is the author of many other titles in the Bookworms series, as well as other nonfiction and early reader books. She lives in Burlington, Connecticut, with her husband and two children.

With thanks to the Reading Consultants:

Nanci Vargus, Ed.D., is an Assistant Professor of Elementary Education at the University of Indianapolis.

Beth Walker Gambro is an Adjunct Professor at the University of Saint Francis in Joliet, Illinois.

Marshall Cavendish Benchmark
99 White Plains Road
Tarrytown, New York 10591-9001
www.marshallcavendish.us

Library of Congress Cataloging-in-Publication Data

Rau, Dana Meachen, 1971-
Trains / by Dana Meachen Rau.
p. cm. — (Bookworms: We go!)
Includes index.
Summary: "Describes the physical attributes, different kinds, and purposes of trains"—Provided by publisher.
ISBN 978-0-7614-4081-9
[1. Railroads—Trains—Juvenile literature.] I. Title.
TF148.R38 2009
625.2—dc22
2008042504

Editor: Christina Gardeski
Publisher: Michelle Bisson
Designer: Virginia Pope
Art Director: Anahid Hamparian

Photo Research by Anne Burns Images

Cover Photo by *Photo Edit*/David Young Wolf

The photographs in this book are used with permission and through the courtesy of:
Ottmar Bierwagen: pp. 1, 15, 20BL. *Alamy Images*: p. 3 Stewart Iskow; pp. 7, 20TR ClassicStock;
pp. 11, 20BR Andre Jenny; pp. 13, 21B Profimedia International; pp. 17, 20TL Jeremy Hoare.
Corbis: pp. 5, 21TL TRANSTOCK; pp. 9, 21TR Atlantide Phototravel; p. 19 Mark E. Gibson.

Printed in Malaysia
1   3   5   6   4   2